The Lord Jesus Christ Crushed Satan

Delivered Me from 7 Hours Demonic Possession

CHIKODI ALEXIS AKONOBI

Published by Faunteewrites Limited

Copyright © 2018 by Chikodi Alexis Akonobi.

Chikodi Alexis Akonobi asserts the moral right to be identified as the author of this work in accordance with the copyright, designs and patents Act 1988.

All rights reserved. No part of this publication may be reproduced, stored in a retrieval system, or transmitted, in any form or by any means, electronic, mechanical, photocopying, recording or otherwise, without the prior permission of the copyright owner.

A CIP catalogue record for this book is available from the British Library.

ISBN: 9780993041778.

A Faunteewrites Book.

Unless otherwise indicated, Bible quotations are taken from the Women's Devotional Bible; New International Version. Copyright © 1990, 1994 by Zondervan Publishing House.

CONTENTS

Chapter One: The Beginning 5

Chapter Two: Spiritual Awakening. 11

Chapter Three: Supernatural Events 19

Chapter Four: The Battle Continues. 33

Chapter Five: Final Crucial Messages To You . . . 51

CHAPTER ONE: THE BEGINNING

Mathew 11: 12, "From the days of John the Baptist till now, the Kingdom of heaven has been forcefully advancing, and forceful men lay hold of it."

Mathew 11: 15, "He who has ears, let him hear."

Psalm 50:14-15 "Sacrifice thanks offering to God, fulfill your vows to the Most High, and call upon me in the day of trouble; I will deliver you, and you will honour me".

The events in this book are not fiction or made up; but are a true-life narration of events that happened to me. There is a spiritual battle going on between the Kingdom of God and the kingdom of darkness for each and every person's soul. From birth till death, there is a constant battle between good and evil, between God and satan. We need to be wise and choose the Kingdom of God regardless of persecution, life's struggles or difficulties. As Christians, we are to fight the good fight of faith. *1 Timothy 6: 12, "Fight the good fight of faith. Take hold of the eternal life to which you were called when you made your good confession in the presence of many witnesses."* When you choose God, and choose to do the WILL of God, you are automatically in a spiritual battle with satan. However, do not be worried for the Lord Jesus has defeated satan and the world. *John 16:33, "I have told you these things, so that in me you may have peace. In this world you will have trouble. But take heart! I have overcome the world."*

My testimony is about God's mighty power to save and how Jesus delivered me from demonic possession. While we were yet in sin, Christ died for us; while I was yet in sin, I called on God and He answered me. I was born into a catholic, at the time, family with loving parents and siblings. I have one brother and four sisters but one passed away as a child. My father, though loving, was involved in occultic practices by night and religious activities by day. This was during my childhood years in the 1990s. During this period, I believe that certain covenants were entered into with satan on behalf of the family by my father. I do not judge or condemn my father because I believe whatever he did was done out of ignorance and as he stated, "For protection". Do not be deceived, you can only get true protection by submitting yourself completely to JESUS CHRIST. We have divine protection in Christ only, *Psalm 91:9-12, "If you make the Most High your dwelling – even the Lord, who is my refuge – then no harm will befall you, no disaster will come near your tent. For He will command His angels concerning you to guard you in all your ways; they will lift you up in their hands, so that you will not strike your foot against a stone.* Anything else promised by any demon, evil spirit, witch, spiritist, sorcerer, occultic person or even religious leader that is contrary to Christ will fail. First, we need protection from satan and its evil schemes for man. Secondly, satan cannot protect you from satan; just like satan cannot cast out satan. *Mathew 12:26, "If satan drives out satan, it is divided against itself. How can its kingdom stand?"* Also, worth pointing out is that satan has no free gift. If satan gives you a gift or promises you power or wealth, run to Christ because satan is after you soul. The devil, aka pant or satan cannot protect you from satan; neither can satan protect sinners from the wrath of God. If something seems too good to be true; it probably is too good to be true! The only exception is salvation, which is a gift from God.

My father attended these occult meetings with the family, which started from around 11pm to about 5am. At about midnight, a spirit was invoked which was addressed as "mother". I believe that spirit is the queen of the coast. Each member brought their concerns to this spirit, in return for sacrifices of some sort to the spirit. Sometimes money and food items were given to the occult leader, other times animals were sacrificed. A few times, I overheard my mom confront my dad about a live ram which was buried in our home as sacrifice to these spirits. More importantly, I believe that covenants were entered into with the kingdom of darkness in exchange for worldly riches, power etc. The sad part is that these covenants go with curses which are passed from generation unto generation. In other words, people sold their souls and those of their children and future generations to the devil in exchange for worldly riches and pleasures. *Mark 8:36-37, "What good is it for a man to gain the whole world, yet forfeit his soul? Or what can a man give in exchange for his soul?"* My family was dedicated to these spirits in exchange for wealth, "protection" and powers. My mother was always against my dad taking the family to these meetings. Her opposition caused a lot of problems between her and my dad but she eventually gave in either to save the marriage or she got weary. Husbands, Wives, parents and children, do not give in to evil just to save a marriage, a job or a family member; by so doing you are choosing that job or marriage or person over the Lord Jesus Christ.

In Mathew 10: 34-39, "Do not suppose that I have come to bring peace to the earth. I did not come to bring peace, but a sword. For I have come to turn "'a man against his father, a daughter against her mother, a daughter-in-law against her mother-in-law — a man's enemies will be the members of his own household.'

"Anyone who loves their father or mother more than me is not worthy of me; anyone who loves their son or daughter more than me is not worthy of me; and anyone who does not take his cross and follow me is not worthy of me. Whoever finds his life will lose it, and whoever loses his life for my sake will find it."

At one of such meetings, this spirit went round each member addressing issues and supposedly "blessing" each person. My siblings were given pills, as they later revealed because the room was always pitch black with no visibility. When the spirit came to me, it tapped me on the chest a few times and moved on to the next person. I did not think much of that since the 1990s till 2011. I still don't know exactly what that meant but I believe it is significant to the events that are discussed in further pages. Still at my childhood years, I had a dream one night that I also think is significant to the events that are unfolding in my life today. I saw JESUS CHRIST, sitting in a circle with his children with his back to me. I touched him; he turned to me and shivered as though power had gone out of him. Next, I saw myself washing my clothes in a basin of water. *Revelation 22:14 "Blessed are those who wash their robes, that they may have the right to the tree of life and may go through the gates into the city.* I don't remember anything else. I believe that the spirit felt the power of God over my life when it tapped me. I also believe that God revealed himself to me first as a child, letting me know of the events that are happening in my life today which had already been predestined by God Himself. I believe that Jesus let me know that I would call on Him, He would answer me, He would wash my sins and every evil covenant away. As I grew older, my dad stated that he gave his life to Christ and we no longer attend these meetings. Throughout my childhood to adult years, I tried to get close to God but there was always something that drew me away from him such as worldly pressures and pleasures. There was no spiritual activity brought to my awareness since then till I was 27 years old.

CHAPTER TWO: SPIRITUAL AWAKENING

I moved to Canada in 2003 to study nursing, graduated in 2008 and started working as a registered nurse. Life seemed good, and without unusual stress. I got married in 2009 to a man whom I thought was a loving and caring husband. We travelled to different places for vacations, not because we were overly wealthy but we were comfortable. I was so grateful to God for giving me a "perfect" husband; or so I thought. He was "too good to be true"; at a point I even compared him to God. I ask God for forgiveness for comparing man to God, for none can compare to God. There is NO duplication of God. I soon realized that the man I married, whom I thought was perfect, was in fact an agent of satan. The biggest tactic of satan is deception and satan uses the most innocent and subtle means, devices or people to achieve its deceptive goals. Life seemed perfect for a period of time.

Suddenly in 2011, strange things started happening around me. It all began when I started noticing my co-workers were intentionally trying to get me angry or upset for reasons unknown to me. What caught my attention was a comment made by a colleague regarding a silent prayer I made to God. I said this prayer in private in my mind, no one else should have known about it except God and me. Somehow it was known by this individual and it did not stop there. I started hearing conversations I made in private with my husband at work. It was so strange to me that I thought my car and home was bugged. I discussed this with my husband but he brushed me off by telling me my coworkers have more important things to do than to bug our car and house. I tried to not think about it but the strange comments continued and even got worse. To the point where I noticed I was being followed by a man. I became curious and concerned because I had made a complaint at work about how my colleagues were behaving toward me; I thought maybe they were mad at me and now they were following me. I started investigating the strange events. Prior to these incidents, I had no issue with anyone; I always kept a quiet profile. I prayed to God about my coworkers and God answered. There were times when my colleagues had planned mischief for me at work, and I could literally feel the presence of God with me during those times.

The strange events soon shifted from work to my home. Still ignorant of the depth and seriousness of the events that were about to unfold, I realized that my husband had everything to do with my predicament at work. Realizing the source of my problem at work, I dropped the complaint at work and resigned from that job in September 2011. I had been praying to God about the situation at work but once God revealed the problem was from my home, I started praying even more to God and did not even worry about my work anymore. I realized this was not a physical battle, but a spiritual one that ONLY GOD can handle; though I still did not know how deeply spiritual the battle was about to get. ***Ephesians 6:12, "For our struggle is not against flesh and blood, but against the rulers, against the authorities, against the powers of this dark world and against the spiritual forces of evil in the heavenly realms."***

2 Corinthians 10:3-4, "For though we live in the world, we do not wage war as the world does. The weapons we fight with are not the weapons of the world. On the contrary, they have divine power to demolish strongholds. I was hurt because I did not expect my husband to have such ill plans for me. I was curious, and wanted to know how my supposedly quiet husband was able to influence my colleagues at work. I thought he worked for an undercover agency, which he did; except it was not one of this world. He was in fact an agent of satan, just as my coworkers were too, hence his influence on my colleagues. This is a fact that was revealed to me by God.

Every event that happens here on earth has a spiritual influence or foundation to it. Do not be deceived, do not be ignorant. There are spiritual forces behind every activity of life, activities at your place of work, your grocery store, your family, your health etc. Angels and demons are constantly at work and at war. The demons influence bad things, like illnesses, accidents and angels protect us from these evil activities. I became aware of this fact as my spiritual senses began to be awakened. There are spirit beings walking among us. When you pray in your mind or think, these spirits can hear you. Hence, my co-workers (who are agents of satan) could pick up on things the normal human being could not. Sometimes, these spirit beings actually speak into your mind and put thoughts in your mind. These are the same spirits that put suicidal thoughts into the minds of individuals or self-destructive thoughts. It is no wonder Paul wrote in *2 Corinthians 10:5, "We demolish arguments and every pretension that sets itself up against the knowledge of God, and we take captive every thought to make it obedient to Christ."* Sometimes satan and its agents will put thoughts in first person tense "I", so that you think they are your thoughts.

Since I had resigned my job, I was now at home resting from all the psychological stress (which lasted about six months) and praying to God for direction regarding my marriage. For the next three months, God started awakening me spiritually. I was prepared to forgive my husband if he had an extra-marital affair but I was not prepared for the events that had just taken place; neither was I prepared for the events that were yet to occur. I fasted, cried and prayed to God for help, healing and direction. During that time my husband and I were never physically at war with each other. He remained quiet, loving and kind in the physical but there was and still is a severe spiritual battle taking place. We would have conversations about the Bible and life; it would seem as though we agreed but he would make a comment or two that set off red flags in my mind. He would say things like, you are being melted for something good to be created; just like gold is melted in fire. He also told me something was about to happen to me. He once said to me that God uses temptation to punish/correct bad behaviour. My reply to him was, the bible also says woe to him through whom the temptation comes from. God does not use temptation to correct/punish people. Instead, He will sometimes use hardship to chastise His children. This is written in ***Luke 17: 1, Jesus said to his disciples: "Things that cause people to sin are bound to come, but woe to that person through whom they come."*** I was familiar with some aspects of the Bible but I did not know how I came up with that scripture. The Spirit of God spoke through me.

Dear reader, satan and its agents know the Bible from cover to cover and they use it to tempt/deceive people. When Jesus was tempted in the wilderness, satan used scripture as its weapon but Jesus overcame satan's temptation by using the right scriptures for His current circumstances. As Christians, we need to know the Bible and which scripture to use at any given trial, tribulation or temptation. The Bible is the word of God, which is the sword of the spirit and what I call the Christian's WEAPON OF MASS EVIL DESTRUCTION. Just as the Spirit of God helped me and is still helping me today; I pray that the Spirit of God helps you too. As a believer, especially new believers, satan and its agents will do everything they can to turn you from God. My advice to you is that you keep praying to God, God sees and knows all things, trust Him with all your heart and He will DEFINITELY see you through each situation. Even when it seems like the odds are against you, keep praying to and believing God, He will definitely make a way where there seems to be no way. HE IS GOD after all. First, God will not allow anyone to be tempted more than they can handle. Second, God ALREADY has a way of escape for each trial or temptation. *1 Corinthians 10:13, "No temptation has seized you except what is common to man. And God is faithful; He will not let you be tempted beyond what you can bear. But when you are tempted, He will also provide a way out so that you can stand up under it."*

At another one of our (me and my husband) Biblical conversations, I made a comment about how lucifer was one of the most beautiful angels created by God before it rebelled against God. My husband gave me a strange look and started sweating in his palm (I was holding his hand). I thought that was a strange reaction but did not think much of it; I later discovered why he had such a reaction. I continued to fast and pray to God without letting anyone know I was fasting. One day my husband, who was out all day, came home and gave me an angry look saying, "There is a spiritual battle going on. Why are you not eating?" I said nothing to him but thought what a strange comment to make out of nowhere and how did he know that I was fasting. I did not know this at the time, but now I know, praying and fasting causes serious catastrophe in the kingdom of darkness. *James 5:*

16, "Therefore confess your sins to each other and pray for each other so that you may be healed. The prayer of a righteous man is powerful and effective." Isaiah 58 also discusses the way we should fast to God. God hears your prayers, prayer is the key; it is the Christian's means of communicating with God. We are to pray in season and out of season. Whatever you do, ALWAYS pray to God regardless of your situation; happy, sad, day or night.

My First Revealed Encounter with Jesus as an Adult

After about a month of staying home without working, struggling with what to do about my marriage due to the betrayal and hurt I was feeling. I decided to go back home to Nigeria for a change of scenery. I can only imagine how hurt God must have been when satan rebelled against him or when each and every one of us sins against God. I discussed my plans with my parents who were in Nigeria; they would always say get your husband's blessings before you travel. It was always said in such a way as though my husband was God and my spirit was unreceptive to that attitude. I was respectful to my husband and I discussed my plans with him but there was this tone of worship that my parents attributed to my husband which was very repulsive to me. I would always tell them that my husband is only man, not God and would be given the respect due to man nothing more.

I decided to purchase my ticket one day, so I sat in front of the computer to book a flight from Canada to Nigeria. Suddenly I felt intense weakness, as though life was being sucked out of me. I could not finish the transaction so I decided to go and lie down. I dragged myself to the couch; put my iPod ear plugs in my ears, and started listening to the gospel songs playing. As I walked to the couch I said a short prayer, **"Into thy hands I commit my spirit. Lord Jesus, receive my soul".** God hears our prayers!!! I fell asleep almost immediately. In my dream, I was on a table surrounded by some people. It was a weird room with candles, like an occult room. I could not see their faces but one of the people had a knife and was about to stab me. Suddenly a light left my body and was in the hand of Jesus (which I believe was my soul). I woke up at that point and the weakness quickly left my body. My iPod started playing a song by Bishop T.D Jakes "Woman Thou Art Loosed". I must mention that this song was in a section of my iPod which I was not aware of. I did not even know that song was on my iPod. I believe the Lord Jesus turned it on to send me a simple but strong message, "Woman thou art loosed!!!" Glory to God!! Unfortunately, I did not get the message at that time. I sat on the couch wondering what the dream and weakness was all about. I wondered if someone wanted to kill me and Jesus saved me. At that moment satan started speaking into my mind, with the following thoughts "God does not exist. God is not real." Thank God for the teaching I have heard since childhood about God. I know that God exists and did not believe any of satan's lies about God. ***Proverbs 22:6, "Train up a child in the way he should go, and when he is old he will not turn from it."*** However, God's existence would only become more REAL to me.

CHAPTER THREE: SUPERNATURAL EVENTS

Strange Events at a Supposedly "Christian" Class

I ended up not purchasing my ticket but decided I will purchase it another day. With everything going on in my life; I desperately needed to draw strength from God by reading my Bible and praying. My husband had advised me to not just read my Bible and pray but to attend Christian programs and courses. He recommended I attend a supposedly Christian course called "Alpha Course" at the church he attends, the Heart Lake Baptist Church in Brampton, Canada. The first day was fairly strange as far as the attitude of those who attended but fairly normal as far as the teaching went. It seemed Biblical and I enjoyed the teaching, ignoring the strange attitudes. The second day I attended was really strange in all aspects of it. The individual facilitating that class started by reading out a statistic of how many churches were owned by satan and how many had agents of satan in them, though not owned by satan; as well as the activities of satan in other areas of life. He read the statistics with so much pride and joy as though he was glorifying satan. I thought that was strange but ignored it. Then someone else stood up and read a joke, all the while looking at me, about how an individual was hanging off a cliff and called to God. God answered and the individual said, "Is anybody there?" In other words, the person did not believe the response from God. My dream immediately came to my mind and I realized for sure Jesus did save me that evening. The dream was not just a dream but had happened in the spiritual realm.

Next, they started singing a gospel song, as soon as I started singing with everyone their faces suddenly looked sad and they stopped the music in the middle of the song! At this point, I knew there was something not quite right with this gathering but I stayed anyway. When they finished the teaching part and got to the discussion part of the class; a lady said, "You will see yourself in another country but you will not know how you got there." I knew from my father's involvement in the occult that she was talking about astral travel and that was definitely not of God. Then she said, "You will start praying but you will fall asleep. You may be wondering why we are doing this. We just want to be sure". I said to myself, "This would be the last time I would attend this course." The class ended shortly after her comments. I went home and shared the teaching part of the course with my husband but said nothing about the strange events and comments. I went to sleep that night listening to gospel songs on my iPod.

My Second Revealed Encounter with Jesus and Deliverance from Demonic Possession

In the morning of September 25, 2011, my husband and I had just finished being intimate with each other. Suddenly, I started behaving like a cat, my tongue was coming in and out of my mouth like a snake, I was not in full control of my body. I was very confused and did not know what was happening. My husband and I started communicating telepathically, we were not speaking out words but he could hear my thoughts and vice versa. I tried listening to my iPod with gospel music playing but it felt like a thousand pins were all over my body. I could not stand it so I threw it on the bed. We went to the bathroom to brush our teeth; it was there that my husband introduced himself as lucifer (telepathically), as satan was in him. Then my husband verbally spoke to me saying, "Are you ok?" I said yes, but I really was not. I lied and that was wrong. This explained his reaction to my comments about lucifer in the previous chapter. I was bent at the waist and thought, why am I not able to stand up? At that moment I stood up; whatever had me bent spiritually let me go. I asked telepathically, knowing that this thing or these things want to torture me, "How come you are obeying me?" He replied, "Because Jesus is in you". We went back to the bedroom, and lay on the bed; I felt this feeling of dread, sorrow and sadness. Telepathically, satan communicated through my husband saying, "We have no time. There is no time". I had all kinds of questions in my thoughts like what is happening? Is it going to be better? My husband turned to me and said audibly, "Keep it simple. Whatever is happening, keep it simple". I got up from the bed, and I felt pain in my left ankle. It was so painful that I had to lie on the floor; I was on my back with my hands and feet in the air like a cat. I thought to myself, I will go back home (Nigeria) and get a strong pastor to cast this thing out of me. My husband then looked at me with a frown and said, "If that is your plan". Then I felt peace in my right side and I could see a figure in my right side. It is hard to explain but there was a being in my right side. My husband started saying to me, "Jesus is in you. Jesus is in you." It was then I realized that the being was JESUS! Even though JESUS was in me, I did not realize what powers were available to me to cast that thing out.

The phone rang, my husband answered; while he was on the phone I touched the phone and I could hear what was being said. I had supernatural powers! My husband pushed me off but I heard the caller say "test her". My husband came back to me after the call and continued saying, "Jesus is in you" in a very nonchalant manner. I was confused and I asked, "How come you can say His name"; as I could no longer say JESUS. He ignored me but dragged me to the living room and said we will watch the gospel of John. We had watched the gospel of John in the past without any problem or strange reaction but that day was different. When he turned it on I was bothered by it. I was uncomfortable anytime the name JESUS was mentioned or even "HE" referring to Jesus or God. I looked at my husband and said who are you? I asked him this question not because I did not know he was my husband but because I had just discovered that there was more to him than meets the eye. He said I am a Christian (such a lie, the devil is a liar!!). I asked, "Why are you doing this?". He said, "I am blessing you"; yet another lie!! The gospel of John bothered me so much that the demons that had entered my body that morning growled at him. He continued holding me tightly and said, "Growl all you like". I vomited and my husband stood up to go clean it; I went and turned the gospel of John off. I was still standing, when suddenly I said **JESUS**! Immediately, my knees were forced to the ground in a kneeling position. I started crying and saying, "I am not worthy, Lord". I glanced at my husband and saw him at the corner looking very disgusted at me.

Dear reader, it is VERY TRUE that at the name of JESUS every knee must bow and every tongue must confess that Jesus Christ is Lord! ***Philippians 2:8-11"And being found in appearance as a man, He humbled Himself and became obedient to death – even death on a cross! Therefore, God exalted Him to the highest place and gave Him the name that is above every name, that at the name of Jesus every knee should bow, in heaven and on earth and under the earth, and every tongue confess that Jesus Christ is Lord, to the glory of God the Father."*** It is also true that the name of the Lord is a strong tower; the righteous run into and are safe. ***Proverbs 18:10, "The name of the Lord is a strong tower; the righteous run to it and are safe."*** After a few minutes of confessing Jesus is Lord, I started binding demons. My husband said, "Stop binding demons, it is gone". I believe my prayer was bothering him. I called a pastor and asked for prayers. I did not tell him exactly what was going on but my husband took the phone from me and said, "She says there are demons in her. I have called others". He looked very arrogant while he spoke. I decided I was not going to stay in that house anymore to entertain anymore evil plans he had in mind. I told my husband I was going out and didn't know when I would be back. I got into my car and started driving, with nowhere in mind but to just get away from my husband. This event started at about 7am and I left the house at about 2pm the same day. It did not last long but it was enough to change my life forever!!! I thought to myself, Jesus actually knows me out of this huge world!!! He actually exists!!! I always believed that Jesus existed but this experience made Him ever so real to me. He actual came to save me!!! Yes, Jesus exists. Yes, He knows each and every one of our names. He created the earth and everything in it. Yes, He came to save each and every one of us; He died for us!!! Accept His love and receive Him into your life; He is calling you today!!!

As I drove on the highway, spirit beings started attacking me and my car. I started speaking in tongues. Speaking in tongues is when the Holy Spirit speaks through a human in a heavenly or foreign language. It is powerful in pulling down evil strongholds and situations. At a point my car started making funny sounds like it was going to stop. I rebuked the evil spirits affecting my car and commanded them to depart from my car. The sound stopped and my car continued fine. I eventually got to the US border; this happened in eastern Canada. I had my passport with a valid US visa of 10 years but the border officials denied me access. I told them I wanted to board a flight from the US as I was unable to board from Canada at that time, which was the truth. The flights from Canada to Nigeria were booked for that day when I last checked online. The officials detained me for about 3 hours, asking me if I had a fight with my husband and I should tell them what my plan was. I told them I just wanted to board a flight and they were welcome to escort me to the airport if they wished. During this 3 hours detention, they had me locked up in a small cell at the boarder; I remembered Paul and Silas from the bible and started singing praises to God. About 1 minute after I started singing, they quickly brought me out, kept asking me what my plan was and if I had a fight with my husband. My song scared them, because they thought the Lord will send an earthquake like He did for Paul and Silas. Finally, I got tired of being asked the same questions repeatedly and I asked to be released so that I can go back to Canada; if they won't let me board a flight from the US. They eventually released me and one of the officials said go home to your husband. There are agents of satan everywhere, in positions of authority, in churches, in government etc. There are also Christians, who are way more powerful spiritually, everywhere also.

As I drove back to Canada from the US border, flashes of lightening started to appear in the sky. I rebuked the demons and commanded the lightening to stop, which it did. By this time, it was about 9pm. I noticed I had a lot of missed calls on my phone, my husband, mother-in-law, dad, sister etc. My brother-in-law called me and said "We were worried about you". So, I called my husband and he said he was worried about me; he said he had filed a missing person's report. I was only gone a few hours, I told him before I left that I did not know when I will be back. So, I could not understand why he called the cops and reported me missing. It is normal protocol for the police not to file a missing person's report until the person has been gone for 24 hours. So, it was strange that they honored my husband's missing person's report. Clearly, he was trying to stop me from leaving the country. I told him I was ok but will not be back that night. I parked at a gas station and spent the night in my car. I kept praying till I fell asleep in my car. In the morning, I drove home; showered and drove off again. I did not want to be around my husband after knowing he tried to invoke a legion of demons to possess my body. I slept in the car, out of town, a second night. By morning, I decided I was going to travel back to Nigeria as I could not keep sleeping in the car.

A Series of Shocking Discoveries:

I booked my flight to Abuja, Nigeria; which was where my mom lived. It was a two-part flight with a lot of strange activities. On the first segment, I felt someone pushing on my thigh but when I opened my eyes there was no contact between me and the lady sitting beside me. By this time, I was already aware that there was something spiritual going on, so I was not scared or bothered. I looked out of the window and I noticed a strange light on the wing of the plane. This light was not the plane's usual light as I was sitting in a section of the plane which was behind the wing; this light was angled directly at me. As I tried shutting the window, I felt a mixture of heat, pain and a force resisting me. I succeeded in closing the window and fell asleep shortly after that. In between the two flight segments I had a few hours waiting period. As I walked to go get some food, my hand luggage suddenly felt 50 pounds heavier and my shoulder felt as though someone was pulling on it. I looked around but could see no one but I would shake it off and feel normal for a few minutes and the weight will come back. The time came for me to board the second flight to Abuja. While on the plane, I felt as though someone was standing on my thigh/leg and I started getting numb/tingly. When I moved, the pressure left but returned later. I realized that I was surrounded by agents of satan who had the ability to get out of their physical body and move about in their spirit being. I looked up and saw a lady standing a couple of rows ahead of me with a ring that had a light shining from it; she was pointing it at me and looking at me. There was no disguise; she did not care if I knew what she was doing. I started praying and listening to gospel music on my iPod. She immediately got very uncomfortable and sat down, the pressure and numbness to my leg soon stopped. As long as I was listening to gospel music on my iPod, I had no more attacks or strange events happen till I got to Abuja. *The first shocking discovery was the ability of these people to leave their physical body. The second pleasantly shocking discovery was the supernatural power of praying, praising God and gospel songs.* I remembered how uncomfortable I was, when I tried to listen to gospel songs while the legion of demons was still in my body. So, I was not surprised. However, I was pleasantly surprised that when I have my iPod on; demons can hear the gospel music.

My dad picked me up from the airport and we went to my mom's house in Abuja. I was washing the dishes and I noticed that the dishes I already washed would have food smeared on them. The first time I washed the dish off, thinking I missed a spot. But then it happened two more times in the same spot I washed. I realised someone was smearing food particles on the clean dishes; though no one was close to me. I was home alone with my mom at that time. I wondered if my own mother was also an agent of satan; possessing the same powers as those on the plane and at the airport. I brushed the thought off. My first night in Abuja, I could not sleep; I was reading the Bible and listening to gospel songs on my iPod in my room. The following morning my mother came out of her room looking very angry at me; she said why didn't you sleep last night? I was surprised that she knew this as we were in separate rooms and I was quiet. By approximately 11am, I fell asleep but was wakened by sounds that was very similar to the one made by the spirit which was invoked in the cult meetings my dad took the family to during my childhood days. I went back to sleep all most immediately after hearing this awful sound. I was awakened again by my mother screaming and saying there was a problem with the pump/tap/faucet at the kitchen sink. She was in a panic and looked both nervous and angry at me. All this time, I could not understand what was going on; but I knew something was happening in the spiritual realm. The second night in Abuja, I tried sleeping but I felt weird sensations from my waste to my toes. I got up and started praying and started singing praises to God. My body started shaking, I started praying and singing even louder; this lasted till about 5am. I got tired and went to sleep. Later in the day after I woke up, my mom came to me and said, "Yesterday was very violent. You really are Jesus's baby". I did not reply her comment, rather I started preaching to her and my dad; I was also prophesying.

The third day in Abuja, I continued reading the bible, listening to gospel music via my iPod and singing praises to God. By evening, my mom asked me to reduce my voice which I did; but she went on to ask me to be medicated. My mother, who claims to be a Christian, said I was sick because I was singing praises to God. When I refused, she called 3 young men to carry me into the car and forced me to go to a clinic with her. When we arrived at the clinic, they attempted to sedate me via injection but the Lord did not permit that. The devil, aka pant or satan can only go as far as God permits. I felt the Spirit of God while we were in the clinic. My mom was ordering the young men to seize me so that I could be injected, but the young men stood helplessly. Then my mother said, "Mmm the spirit is weak". God weakened them, Glory to God!!! So, we went back to my mother's house without me being sedated. *The third shocking discovery is that even my family members, though claiming to be Christians, are involved in satanic activities.* By the third day, my mom was really uncomfortable with my reading the Bible and listening to gospel music. I decided to leave my mom's house since she said I made her very uncomfortable. She went on to call four young men again to force me into her car; she drove me to the hospital in Abuja and asked to be seen by a psychiatrist. These were her reasons: I was praying loudly, I was prophesying, I was singing praises to God and I never did those before. The psychiatrists kept asking me if her comments were true and why. They wanted to know if I had problems with my husband. I refused to speak with them because I knew their plan. They went on to sedate me forcefully. Though no diagnosis was made; the psychiatrists "queried" psychosis and gave me a lot of sedatives usually given to individuals diagnosed with schizophrenia. *The devil is a liar; when they (satan and its agents) can't control you, they try to convince you that you are crazy or keep you sedated and weak. The fourth shocking discovery is that the devil has agents across the globe, in various positions to try and torture Christians or hinder the ministry of God.*

I was in the hospital for about 3 or 4 days, constantly being sedated. I could no longer stand it, so I walked out of the hospital without being discharged and being very drowsy. The Lord had helped me walk out of the hospital, even though they positioned an armed military man at the entrance of the unit. It was a miracle!!! I went back to my mom's house; having nowhere else to go to in Abuja and my bag was with my mom. My mom allowed me to stay in her house only if I agreed to be medicated. I said yes, but I never took the pills. I always pocketed them in my mouth and later flushed them down the toilet. My husband eventually came to Abuja from Canada. My mom, my husband and I went to the hospital again at my mom's request. This time my husband said to me, "If you cooperate, they will let you go". The doctors asked me the same questions over and over; I answered the questions. Then the psychiatrist, having read my mind, asked me what my plan was. I said when I get to Canada I would leave my husband. With that response, she ordered a stronger sedative which lasted a month in my system and took another month to clear from my body. During this period, I had a lot of nightmares. She said there was a "chemical imbalance" in my system, because I wanted to leave my husband. The medication affected my motor function, restricting my movement. That was satan's way of preventing me from leaving my mom's house or my husband; but when the spirit of God is in you, satan CANNOT stop you. My husband and I went back to Canada together; I agreed to be seen by a psychiatrist in Canada. I was seen by the psychiatrist for about three months, each visit I considered a complete waste of my time. However, I went for the visits as I agreed to do so. I was asked the same questions over and over again. Why were you praying loudly? Why did you leave your husband's house on September 25th without your husband's permission and without telling him where you were going to? Why do you wake up in the middle of the night and start praying? You were not this prayerful, why the change in your prayer life? My response was always the same, "I became born again and started getting closer to God, hence the change. I was very much aware of what I was doing on September 25th when I left the house. I wanted to be away from my husband. I wake up in the middle of the night to pray when the need arises (In those situations, I had bad dreams, I was being attacked spiritually through dreams so I woke up and prayed to God; cancelling the work of satan and its agents against my life). I prayed loudly as needed, sometimes Jesus gave commands to spirits or prayed to God in a loud voice. It is not uncommon for members of my church to pray in a loud voice, that is not a symptom of mental illness."

Not one single reason presented by the doctors, my husband or my mom is a symptom of mental illness. Rather, these are manifestations of being born again. The Bible tells us that when a person becomes born again "old things are passed away, behold all things become new". *2 Corinthians 5:17, "Therefore, if anyone is in Christ, he is a new creation; the old has gone, the new has come!"* You become a new creature; you start to desire the things of God. You pray always, in all situations, with all kinds of prayers. Your old ungodly habits fade away; if you were a gambler, you do not desire to gamble anymore. You desire to read your Bible always; you sing praises to God for His marvellous love and mercy. The psychiatrist in Canada agreed that none of those activities were a symptom of mental illness; she went on to say that she was concerned because my family members were concerned. Dear reader, the Bible tells us that we cannot be greater than our master Jesus. *John 13:16, "I tell you the truth, no servant is greater than his master, nor is a messenger greater than the one who sent him".* If Jesus was persecuted, scorned, insulted, accused of being demon possessed and mentally ill; so also, shall we go through the same things. *John 10:20, "Many of them said, He is demon-possessed and raving mad. Why listen to him? John 15:18, "If the world hates you, keep in mind that it hated me first."*

Mathew 10: 24-25, "A student is not above his teacher, nor a servant above his master. It is enough for the student to be like his teacher, and the servant like his master. If the head of the house has been called Beelzebub, how much more the members of His household! If Jesus, being God but came to earth as a mere mortal man, was able to endure till the end and finish his purpose for coming to earth by God's grace; so also, shall we finish our purpose here on earth by God's grace. *John 19:30, "When He had received the drink, Jesus said," It is finished". With that He bowed His head and gave up His spirit."*

CHAPTER FOUR:
THE BATTLE CONTINUES

God is omniscience (all knowing), he knows our thoughts even before they are formed and the end from the beginning; satan is not omniscience. Though satan and its agents can hear your thoughts, they DO NOT know God's plan for Christians and the ministries of God. Hence, they are constantly fishing for information via various means including but not limited to, reading your mind, using random strangers to ask seemingly innocent questions, using family members, friends, teachers, police officers, government officials etc. As mentioned earlier, I was seen by the psychiatrist in Canada for about three months with no definite diagnosis and no further medications. I was just asked a lot of questions, fishing for my thoughts and plans. One day my husband asked me what I thought about the whole events starting in September 25, 2011; the hospitalization, the dreams. I said nothing. He went on to say, you were gradually getting close to God and all of a sudden you sprang up. So, I said to him, "why is it that you have been telling me to get close to God, now I am getting close to God you all fight me and say I am psychotic?" He replied, "You think the devil is going to wait….". He did not finish his sentence and changed the subject. I eventually started working in December 2011, still living with my husband; I held two part-time positions at two different facilities. I continued to build my relationship with God by praying, fasting, listening to gospel music, praising God, reading the bible or listening to the bible (audio bible).

As I did this, my gentle and quiet husband started getting very hostile toward me. He called me names and said "everyone hates you". I could not relate to his comment, as I was not aware of anyone that hated me, till later. Apparently, my praying, fasting and praising God was disturbing satan and its agents (including my husband). He tried everything he could to put out the Spirit of God in me but he was unsuccessful and remains unsuccessful. My husband asked me to go to his church and speak with a couple of people who he claimed had experience with demons. I refused knowing that the demonic activity that manifested in my life was linked to my attending the Alpha Course in that same church. My husband even said so himself. I did, however, try to reach various pastors for prayers; I was still learning the word of God. I went to speak with Pastor T from Redeemed Church, House of Praise in western Canada. After telling her my story and experience with the demon possession, and how Jesus delivered me; she said, "Jesus did not do anything for you. Why are you still with your husband?" I told her that God was against divorce and I did not want to offend God. She said, "not in your situation". Dear reader, it is very dangerous to go from church to church seeking prayers; this is because MANY churches may appear to be from God but are operating with demonic powers. My advice to anyone in need, in trouble, seeking help is that you should get on your knees and pray directly to God! You can never go wrong and God will DEFINITELY answer your honest prayers!!! While it is good to seek help from genuine pastors of God; satan has planted many false prophets in every nook and cranny of the world. If you do not have the spirit of discernment, you will fall for their tricks; and end down worse than before.

I was advised by friends and my husband to go for deliverance. The mental illness lies were no longer used to explain the strange events at that time. My family members finally agreed this was a spiritual battle not a physical or medical battle. However, they were wrong in asking me to seek deliverance; because Jesus said in ***John 8:36, "So if the Son sets you free, you will be free indeed."*** Jesus, Himself set me free on September 25th 2011; and **HE WHOM THE SON HAS SET FREE, IS FREE INDEED!!! I WAS SET FREE IN THE NAME OF JESUS. THAT NAME "JESUS" IS SUCH A MARVELOUS MYSTERY; LET THE NAME "JESUS" ALWAYS BE ON YOUR LIPS, THOUGH NOT AS A CUSS WORD!!!** I do not need any further deliverance done other than the one done by Christ Himself!!! Praise be to God!!! Glory to God!!! Hallelujah!!! I am free because of that name JESUS!!! I have learned from my experiences, to go DIRECTLY to God in prayers if I have any need, concern, request or thanks offering. My prayer life and relationship with God continues to grow and be strengthened. One day, while I was singing gospel songs and listening to my iPod; I looked out of the window and in the sky was a large dark cloud which formed a skull. The skull was faced towards me; I looked in the socket area where the eyes are supposed to be and said, "I am not afraid of you. Greater is He that is in me than he that is in you". Within seconds, the cloud cleared; and I continued to praise and worship God.

By January 2012 I realized I was a target for satan and its agents; this was no surprise to me. When you choose to do the will of God, satan will attack you in any way, shape or form; in an attempt to put the fire of God out in you and stop the ministry of

God. But God is faithful and just, He always protects His children and whatever ministry He has called them to. We can see this throughout the Bible but I especially like to refer to the life of apostle Paul. Apostle Paul, formerly used by satan to persecute and even kill Christians, was called by God to a ministry of reconciliation (reconciling men to God), planting churches and making apostles of men. Throughout his ministry, satan attacked him in various forms (using fellow citizens, men in authority, nature-hurricane and snake), he was imprisoned, beaten, shipwrecked, bitten by a snake etc. He lived to tell the story; he did not die till he finished his purpose and ministry. To attack a Christian or the ministry of God is to contend with God; no one can successfully contend with God. I was and still am being attacked by satan and its agents; but God has seen me through and continues to see me through each attack. **Psalm 34:19, "A righteous man may have many troubles, but the Lord delivers him from them all."**

I came to work one day and what I felt is difficult to explain. It felt like a massive headache plus my whole body was being pulled all over by unseen forces. I saw some guests visiting some patients looking at me and smiling in an evil way; some of the staff were looking at me in a strange way, some looked irritated, some looked angry and some just went about their business like normal. I was in agony and I realized that I was being attacked by the people around me (co-workers, visitors and patients) in the spirit form. This lasted the entire shift; but half way into the shift I got my iPod and started listening to gospel music. This stopped the agony; all the spirit beings left me each time I listened to gospel music through my iPod. There is power in singing praises to God, even if you do so in your mind. The next day the same thing happened but at my second job. This time I did not have the iPod but the Spirit of God came upon me and I started speaking in tongues. This deterred the spirits of my coworkers and I could see some of them in physical agony. I overheard one staff say to the other, "what is this? She is speaking in tongues? How is this?" I gave God glory because again he provided a way of escape. This time I continued speaking in tongues till I got home. When I got home at about midnight, I felt the ground shake a bit and there were a lot spirits in the house. These are human beings that were able to leave their bodies via evil powers. Probably there were demons present as well. These spirit beings started attacking me; I continued speaking in tongues and I had my hands out as though pushing something away (motioning it in a circle round me). This kept the spirits away from me; God had sent help, AS ALWAYS, as the spiritual battle continued.

After about an hour the attacks stopped and the spirits started speaking through me with different voices and accents. One of the voices said, I was the one who made you finish quickly at work. Another asked if I was not tired yet and that I should ask God to send a stronger angel to help me. Another said we will deal with you before you enter that throne of grace. Another said, "You will be a nurse for only 3 more years and you will die at 35yrs old". Another said that that redeemed church house of praise that I went to was from the devil. Another started talking about my fasting and how I did not need to fast as God has already answered my prayers (I planned on going on three days dry fast). The devil is a liar, the fasting was actually causing trouble in the kingdom of darkness and they wanted me to stop fasting. Another claimed to be an angel and asked me to go and eat; claiming that by eating and nourishing my body, I had entertained an angel unknowingly. This was a lie as I later discovered. This spirit said that my husband, who was at work at the time, would come back in tears of repentance. This was just another lie as my husband did come back, but he was far from tears. He was in fact very arrogant and unrepentant. By this time, I was in the process of relocating from east to west. I didn't like living in eastern Canada and decided to relocate; my husband refused to relocate and still resides in eastern Canada. One of the spirits that spoke through me introduced itself as my mother-in-law, saying that my husband will relocate with me, become a pastor and I should support him. The thing said it liked the power it had so that it could deal with people like me who offended it.

Dear reader, when Jesus talks about wide is the way to destruction and narrow is the way to eternal life; He really means it. There are a lot of people being used by satan. It felt like the entire city was involved in satanic activities in one way or another. I could no longer be certain of anyone's true belief, not my family, not even those who claim to be Christians and men of God. I am sure that there are true Christians and men of God around but I can guarantee you that they are a lot fewer than the non-Christians. This is backed up by the Bible. Examples are the story of Sodom and Gomorrah in **Genesis 19**; the entire cities were destroyed with only three people saved, Lot and his two daughters. There were only three people in Sodom and Gomorrah that did the will of God, hence their lives were spared. Another example is the story of Noah; only eight people were saved (Noah, his wife, their three sons and the wives of the three sons). The entire earth was destroyed by flood except for the family of Noah. So, it should not come as a surprise to you when I say a great majority of people living on this earth are not doing the will of God; many are agents of satan, even your family members. It is no wonder Jesus said in **Luke 14: 26, "If anyone comes to me and does not hate his father and mother, his wife and children, his brothers and sisters-yes even his own life – he cannot be my disciple." In Mathew 10: 34-39, "Do not suppose that I have come to bring peace to the earth. I did** *not come to bring peace, but a sword. For I have come to turn "'a man against his father, a daughter against her mother, a daughter-in-law against her mother-in-law — a man's enemies will be the members of his own household.'*

"Anyone who loves their father or mother more than me is not worthy of me; anyone who loves their son or daughter more than me is not worthy of me; and anyone who does not take his cross and follow me is not worthy of me. Whoever finds his life will lose it, and whoever loses his life for my sake will find it.

Later that night I went to sleep and I was attacked in the dream. I was held down by strong arms and surrounded by lots of people but could not see their faces. I tried to wake up but could not wake up. Something was drilled into my right hip and it caused me a lot of pain. I cried to God in the dream saying, "Father help me". Not long after I said those words I woke up and started speaking in tongues; the time was about 0330 am. My husband, who was sleeping in the next room, woke up and said I could not sleep in his house anymore. He said my speaking in tongues was bothering him and the neighbours. I asked him how he knew the neighbours were bothered, I was not loud, they cannot hear me and no one had complained. He stuttered and said, "you just can't sleep here anymore". It was about 0330 am and my loving husband kicked me out of the house. I had nowhere to go so I went downstairs to the car and stayed in the car. Hoping to stay there till daybreak then I can find a hotel to stay for the next four days. My flight to the west was scheduled to depart in four days. While in the car, the attacks continued and I continued to speak in tongues. I felt a force pushing against my hands in a struggle but could see no one. I could see someone from the corner of my eye (my peripheral vision) on several occasions but when I turned no one was there. I saw a man standing a few meters from where the car was parked partially hidden by a tree; his arms were stretched towards my direction but when I looked at him he put his hands down and entered the house. I suddenly started experiencing catarrh (runny nose) and my throat became dry making it uncomfortable for me to speak; that did not stop me from speaking in tongues.

The struggle continued till about 8am, and then my husband asked me to speak to my mom on the phone. She asked me to go see a doctor because my husband told her that I was speaking in tongues. I refused and told my husband that I would leave his house, since he did not want me to stay there anymore. He was angry and called me names; he said I was arrogant and that people were afraid of me. He said, "everyone hates you and you will continue to be attacked". I was not bothered because Jesus said in **John 15:18, "If the world hates you, keep in mind that it hated me first."** Suddenly he became nice to me saying, "We love you and would like you to see a doctor". His plan was to try and sedate me again but God did not permit this to happen a second time. Remember satan can only go as far as God permits it to. When I refused to go see a doctor, he asked me to go to his church with him to see a pastor for deliverance; it was a Sunday morning. I refused to go to church with him, so he went without me. When he came back, he continued to ask me to go see a doctor; my mom called and asked him to force me to the hospital. My husband called the cops and told them to take me to the hospital for psychiatric assessment. While he was still on the phone I left his house, and wanted to find a hotel or change my flight date to travel that day. But the cops called my cell and asked me to meet with them just so they could make sure I was ok. They lied, as is consistent with agents of satan. When they got to where I was waiting for a taxi, I was hand cuffed and driven to the hospital. On the way to the hospital I was speaking in tongues, in a quiet voice, and this bothered the police officer. I could see that he was very restless, uncomfortable and fidgety.

I was admitted to the hospital but I continued to pray to God and speak in tongues. I was not swayed by their stunt to keep me hospitalized. This time I was going to fight back, not physically but by continuous prayers to God. Every time I prayed the nurses will come in and try to scare me by checking my vitals, writing notes in my presence and even telling me they were worried about me. These agents of satan would make my heart beat fast, doing so by leaving their physical bodies as discussed earlier. It recorded on the monitor that my heart rate was 130 beats per minute; and the nurse said to me "your pulse is high as it is with people who are in here". I just laughed at them in my mind and was never scared for I knew God was with me. If God be for us who can be against us? I was put on a form 1, which meant I was to be held in the hospital against my will for up to three days. I was seen by a couple of doctors and psychiatrists; they would ask about me speaking in tongues. I told them I was praying to God and that "I feel sorry for anyone who thinks that speaking in tongues or praying to God is a mental illness." I was asked if I prayed at work and during the hospitalization, I said yes to both. I asked the doctors why they have not hospitalized all the pastors that speak in tongues but they did not respond. I was no longer going to let satan and its agents tie me down. The second day I was hospitalized, my husband came to visit me and I could feel the earth shaking and vibrating as he walked. He said he did not sleep the night before. I laughed and said, "Well I was not at home with you so you cannot blame me for that". He did not say much but then the Spirit of God spoke through me and I said to him, "satan can only go as far as God permits" and I laughed. I also started speaking in tongues to him and he immediately said he had to leave. I was not given a single medication or injection or sedative throughout the hospitalization. There was not even a single note made in my chart by the doctors as I was informed by one of the nurses assigned to me. My husband wanted me out of the house but for some reason he still wanted to be in control of me.

After three days of being hospitalized, I was discharged and I went back to my husband's house for the night as my flight was the next morning. The attacks continued through the night and I continued praising God and listening to gospel music via my iPod. I would feel the bed or the ground vibrate for a split second but I was never bothered. I knew that the agents of satan were present in their spirit beings and trying to scare me. The next day I boarded the flight out west, and while I was on the plane, I fell asleep. Then a spirit spoke through me saying, "Nto gi" in Igbo language which meant "good for you". I perceived that this spirit was my sister. While still in a deep sleep, I felt an angel of God come to my aid and I woke up immediately. Then I started listening to gospel songs via my iPod. I saw passengers on the plane four seats ahead of me turn and give me an angry look. Some of them looked very uncomfortable.

I arrived in western Canada, at my sister's house; I continued praying and fasting. I have been fasting for months at a time, sometimes three days in a row. While at my sister's house I was still being attacked. I would be praying and suddenly feel like vomiting. It was as if someone put their hand in my throat, hence stimulating my gag reflex. I perceived in my spirit that this was my father, though he was physically in Nigeria. Shortly after, my father called me and while speaking to him I felt someone pressing on my head. Later that day I went to the registry to register my vehicle; I continued to pray in my mind. I would think thoughts like swords of fire piercing satan, its demons and agents;

immediately I felt the attack of satan. I felt someone pressing on my head, twisting various muscles in my body causing me discomfort. I noticed a particular man who stood by the door of the registry looking at me with a very serious look; then he would get fidgety, go outside and come back and continue looking at me. This happened a few times till I left the registry. By the second day I was to drive about three hours to my new apartment. As I drove I felt someone holding my head and I would get really sleepy. Once, I almost ran into another car but I felt the presence of God and I woke up immediately.

I arrived at my new apartment in western Canada; then got settled and started my new job at a nearby hospital. At first the staff appeared friendly and normal; but they got very hostile very quickly both physically and spiritually. I would be told to perform a task a certain way, once I did it the way I was told the same person will say no, do it another way. When I asked but you asked me to do it this way, she said yes but it changes. I thought nothing of it but quickly realized that things were being moved around and manipulated to get me upset, frustrated or angry. It never worked as I was determined to have the joy of the Lord. I was attacked in various ways, once I double checked a resident's name and the medication I wanted to administer; it looked accurate only to realize a few minutes later that I was about to give the medication to the wrong person. Sometimes I was hypnotised, I would just perform certain tasks only to realize I had not planned on performing those tasks. It was very strange, but I was not surprised as I was very well aware of the spiritual battle that has been going on for some time now. Sometimes, I would be working on something and my nose will start dripping and stop after two seconds; this happened several times. Sometimes I would feel someone tickling my nose or head or putting stuff in my eyes or various parts of my body;

other times I would feel pain in my internal organs or muscle. Sometimes, someone will put a cookie on my medication cart; because I was constantly fasting and praying. Sometimes, I would be offered food by staff; there was always food everywhere at work and I would be asked to eat something. Sometimes I would perform a task but my memory of performing that task would be wiped out and I would go to repeat the same task only to remember that I had already done it. During this period, one staff would come to me and make a comment about me losing my memory and would laugh. It was an obvious battle, no one was bothered that I was aware of what was going on; neither was I bothered. One particular resident said to me on more than one occasion, "We know all about you. Don't say anything about us to anybody and we won't say anything to anybody about you." I said nothing because, not only will I not be involved in the evil of this world; I will expose the evil activities that God has permitted me to experience. ***Ephesians 5: 11, "Have nothing to do with the fruitless deeds of darkness, but rather expose them." 1 Timothy 5: 20, "Those who sin are to be rebuked publicly, so that the others may take warning." Revelations 12: 11, "They overcame him by the blood of the lamb and by the word of their testimony; they did not love their lives so much as to shrink from death."***

When I go home after work and try to pray or sing praises to God, I am constantly battling with my "thoughts"; as these agents of satan put different thoughts in my mind to distract me from my prayers and praises. It is no wonder Paul said in ***2 Corinthians 10:3-5, "For though we live in the world, we do not wage war as the world does. The weapons we fight with are not the weapons of the world. On the contrary, they have divine power to demolish strongholds. We demolish arguments and every pretension that sets itself up against the knowledge of God, and we take*** lieved God had permitted those events to strengthen my faith. I refused and still refuse to sin against God or be mad at God.

When I went home, I asked God to forgive me of any sin which I may have committed knowingly or unknowingly. I asked Him for the grace to be more like Him and to do His will. Then the following things occurred to me:

1) My position as a nurse was taking up a great majority of my time, hence, distracting me from God and the work of God.

2) I reduced my praying habit; in fact, I stopped praying when I was told that my position was threatened if I did not stop.

3) I had doubted God's awesome power and ability to provide for His children. I had taken my focus away from Him for a short while and focused on my physical effort to try and save my job/ please man.

4) I realized my position as a nurse was a form of a stronghold in my life.

5) I was put in a position where I had to choose between God and money (my Job). I chose God.

6) While I was waiting for the right time to serve God and putting my nursing job/ activities of daily living as a priority over the work of God; souls were perishing daily.

7) NOW is the time to preach and share the gospel of Jesus to the multitudes.

That night I decided to quit my job as a nurse and go into full time ministry. I decided to lay down my full time registered nurse job, the latest model of the range rover evoque and high-class apartment, for the name JESUS by which I am saved; completely and utterly trusting God. I have never lacked a thing. God has moved people and elements on this earth and above to meet my every need.

CHAPTER FIVE:
FINAL CRUCIAL MESSAGES TO YOU

Jesus came to earth and set an example for us with His ministry here on earth, that we should do likewise. *John 13:15, "I have set you an example that you should do as I have done for you"*. I would like to emphasize some points in this single verse.

- It talks about "service". As children of God we are "servants" of God. We are called to serve the Lord in whatever form or way the Lord leads you, as Christ had done for us. It is a call to service.

- It talks about "endurance". Christ was scorned, ridiculed, falsely accused of being demon-possessed and raving mad, physically beaten, literally carried His cross and was crucified; but He endured till the end. We are to endure persecution and persevere as Christ did.

- It talks about "overcoming". As children of God we are more than "overcomers". Christ was tempted by satan in many ways than one. Even using the Bible, satan tempted Jesus.

Christ overcame satan also using the Bible. We are to overcome satan by rebuking satan, using the word of God and holding unto God.

- It talks about "reconciliation". Jesus has a ministry of reconciliation, reconciling men to God. Jesus is still reconciling men to God even TODAY. We are to reconcile men to God, through Christ Jesus by preaching the gospel and declaring the word of God. "REPENT, FOR THE KINGDOM OF GOD IS AT HAND."

- It talks about "moving above betrayal". The devil, aka pant, used the disciple of Jesus as seen with Judas Iscariot, who betrayed Jesus. We may be betrayed by our loved ones or even members of the church, be not discouraged. Jesus was betrayed also, but it did not stop Him from fulfilling His purpose.

- It talks about "fulfilling your purpose in the midst of opposition". Jesus had a purpose and it was to reconcile man to God via the cross. The devil tried to prevent Him from fulfilling this purpose by various means, including using the "chief priests" to challenge His ministry (seen at various parts of the gospel of John), trying to get Him arrested before the appointed time and using His brothers, John 7:3-8. The devil, aka pant, went as far as trying to kill Jesus by crucifying Him, but it only fulfilled God's plan ignorantly. The devil, aka pant, will try to thwart God's plan but will only end up fulfilling God's plan ignorantly.

- It talks about "obedience". Christ was obedient to God the Father, who sent Him to earth for a ministry of reconciliation. He was obedient even when the world was against Him to the point of death; God raised Him up and glorified Him. We are to be obedient to Christ even when the world is against us to the point of death.

John 13:15, "I have set you an example that you should do as I have done for you."

Whatever you do make sure that you hold on to Christ till the end; and snatch people out of the fire. *Jude 1:23, "snatch others from the fire and save them; to others show mercy, mixed with fear--hating even the clothing stained by corrupted flesh."* Let Steven be an example to you, even while he was being stoned he was praying for the people who were stoning him. Let Christ Jesus be the ultimate example, He died for our sins; for the sins of those who crucified Him. While He was being crucified He still prayed for them, enduring till the end. Christ is still interceding on our behalf; He is still saving souls even today! Whatever you do, DO NOT give in to sin and DO NOT give up but hold on to Christ till the end. It may not always be easy, but it is VERY possible by the grace of God. *Mathew 10:38-39, "and anyone who does not take his cross and follow me is not worthy of me. Whoever finds his life will lose it, and whoever loses his life for my sake will find it."*

John 16:33, "I have told you these things, so that in me you may have peace. In this world you will have trouble. But take heart! I have overcome the world."

Finally, **Jesus is coming back** to this earth sooner than expected. With each second that passes by, we are that much closer to his return. The day or the hour is not known by any man or even the angels but by the Father only. Are you ready for his return? **Will you be among the righteous** that will be taken up with Jesus? If you are not sure, now is your opportunity to **be reconciled to**

God. The Bible warns us that the wages of sin is **death, spiritual death, HELL, A LAKE OF FIRE, and TORMENT that LASTS FOR EVER and EVER.** Many will end down in hell, don't be one of them. There is a real battle for the soul of each one of us; it will be foolish not to take heed of these warnings. Now is your opportunity to repent, avoid hell and be reconciled to God. God exists!!! I know this beyond the shadow of a doubt because I have seen and felt His presence and power. Have **FAITH in God**; **BELIEVE** in God's promises. Be of good courage, say the prayer below, mean it and believe that Jesus has answered your prayer:

"Heavenly Father, have mercy on me and forgive me, a sinner. I believe in you and that your word is true. I believe that Jesus Christ is the Son of the living God and that He died on the cross so that I may now have forgiveness for my sins and eternal life. I know that without you in my heart, my life is meaningless.

I believe in my heart that you, Lord God, raised Him from the dead. Please Jesus forgive me, for every sin I have ever committed or done. Please Lord Jesus come into my heart as my personal Lord and Saviour today. I need you to be my Father and my Friend. Please direct my path and lead me through every trial. Please give me your grace to continue this journey with you till the end. I give you my life and ask you to take full control from this moment on. I pray this in the name of Jesus Christ." Amen.

What Next?

If you said the above prayer, CONGRATULATIONS! My advice to you is to do the following:

- Pray to God at all times. Take all your needs, questions, doubts and concerns to God in prayer.

- Praise, thank and worship God at all times, especially when you are going through difficult situations.

- If you commit sin or offend God, ask for God's forgiveness and He will forgive you. Avoid offending God and ask for the Holy Spirit to help you avoid sin.

- Read your Bible; this will strengthen your faith. It will inform you of God's promises and resources that are available to us. It will help you get through ANY situation.

- Find a living and Holy Spirit filled church to attend, some may be available online. Ask God for the spirit of discernment so that you do not fall prey to the false prophets. Though they are fewer, there are still churches that are not from satan as seen in the book of Revelation.

Feel free to contact me at cakonobi@yahoo.com if you need someone to talk to, pray with you; or for questions and comments regarding any content of this book. I can also be reached via YouTube at https://www.youtube.com/chikodialexisakonobi and via Facebook at https://www.facebook.com/chiko.alexis

Bible Quotations

Mathew 11: 12, "From the days of John the Baptist till now, the Kingdom of heaven has been forcefully advancing, and forceful men lay hold of it."

Mathew 11: 15, "He who has ears, let him hear."

Psalm 50:14-15 "Sacrifice thanks offering to God, fulfill your vows to the Most High, and call upon me in the day of trouble; I will deliver you, and you will honour me".

1 Timothy 6: 12, "Fight the good fight of faith. Take hold of the eternal life to which you were called when you made your good confession in the presence of many witnesses."

Psalm 91:9-12, "If you make the Most High your dwelling – even the Lord, who is my refuge – then no harm will befall you, no disaster will come near your tent. For He will command His angels concerning you to guard you in all your ways; they will lift you up in their hands, so that you will not strike your foot against a stone.

Mathew 12:26, "If satan drives out satan, he is divided against himself. How can his kingdom stand?"

Mark 8:36-37, "What good is it for a man to gain the whole world, yet forfeit his soul? Or what can a man give in exchange for his soul?"

In Mathew 10: 34-39, "Do not suppose that I have come to bring peace to the earth. I did not come to bring peace, but a sword. For I have come to turn "'a man against his father, a daughter against her mother, a daughter in-law against her mother-in-law

—a man's enemies will be the members of his own household.'

"Anyone who loves their father or mother more than me is not worthy of me; anyone who loves their son or daughter more than me is not worthy of me; and anyone who does not take his cross and follow me is not worthy of me. Whoever finds his life will lose it, and whoever loses his life for my sake will find it."

Ephesians 6:12, "For our struggle is not against flesh and blood, but against the rulers, against the authorities, against the powers of this dark world and against the spiritual forces of evil in the heavenly realms."

2 Corinthians 10:3-5, "For though we live in the world, we do not wage war as the world does. The weapons we fight with are not the weapons of the world. On the contrary, they have divine power to demolish strongholds. We demolish arguments and every pretension that sets itself up against the knowledge of God, and we take captive every thought to make it obedient to Christ.

Luke 17: 1, Jesus said to his disciples: "Things that cause people to sin are bound to come, but woe to that person through whom they come."

1 Corinthians 10:13, "No temptation has seized you except what is common to man. And God is faithful; He will not let you be tempted beyond what you can bear. But when you are tempted, He will also provide a way out so that you can stand up under it."

James 5: 16, "Therefore confess your sins to each other and pray for each other so that you may be healed. The prayer of a righteous man is powerful and effective."

Proverbs 22:6, "Train up a child in the way he should go, and when he is old he will not turn from it."

Philippians 2:8-11"And being found in appearance as a man, He humbled Himself and became obedient to death – even death on a cross! Therefore, God exalted Him to the highest place and gave Him the name that is above every name, that at the name of Jesus every knee should bow, in heaven and on earth and under the earth, and every tongue confess that Jesus Christ is Lord, to the glory of God the Father."

2 Corinthians 5:17, "Therefore, if anyone is in Christ, he is a new creation: the old has gone, the new has come!"

John 13:16, "I tell you the truth, no servant is greater than his master, nor is a messenger greater than the one who sent him."

John 10:20, "Many of them said, He is demon-possessed and raving mad. Why listen to him?"

John 15:18, "If the world hates you, keep in mind that it hated me first."

Mathew 10: 24-25, "A student is not above his teacher, nor a servant above his master. It is enough for the student to be like his teacher, and the servant like his master. If the head of the house has been called Beelzebub, how much more the members of His household!"

John 19:30, "When He had received the drink, Jesus said," It is finished." With that He bowed His head and gave up His spirit."

John 8:36, "So if the Son sets you free, you will be free indeed."

Psalm 34:19, "A righteous man may have many troubles, but the Lord delivers him from them all."

Luke 14: 26, "If anyone comes to me and does not hate his father and mother, his wife and children, his brothers and sisters-yes even his own life – he cannot be my disciple."

In Mathew 10: 34-39, "Do not suppose that I have come to bring peace to the earth. I did not come to bring peace, but a sword. For I have come to turn "'a man against his father, a daughter against her mother, a daughter-in-law against her mother-in-law — a man's enemies will be the members of his own household.'

"Anyone who loves their father or mother more than me is not worthy of me; anyone who loves their son or daughter more than me is not worthy of me; and anyone who does not take his cross and follow me is not worthy of me. Whoever finds his life will lose it, and whoever loses his life for my sake will find it.

Ephesians 5: 11, "Have nothing to do with the fruitless deeds of darkness, but rather expose them."

1 Timothy 5: 20, "Those who sin are to be rebuked publicly, so that the others may take warning."

Revelation 12: 11, "They overcame him by the blood of the lamb and by the word of their testimony; they did not love their lives so much as to shrink from death."

. Mathew 18:18, "I tell you the truth, whatever you bind on earth will be bound in heaven, and whatever you loose on earth will be loosed in heaven."

John 14:13, "And I will do whatever you ask in my name, so that the Son may bring glory to the Father."

Matthew 5:39-41, "But I tell you, do not resist an evil person. If someone strikes you on the right cheek, turn to him the other cheek. And if anyone wants to sue you and take your tunic, let him have your cloak as well. If someone forces you to go one mile, go with him two miles."

John 13:15, "I have set you an example that you should do as I have done for you".

Jude 1:23, "snatch others from the fire and save them; to others show mercy, mixed with fear--hating even the clothing stained by corrupted flesh."

Mathew 10:38-39, "and anyone who does not take his cross and follow me is not worth of me. Whoever finds his life will lose it, and whoever loses his life for my sake will find it."

John 16:33, "I have told you these things, so that in me you may have peace. In this world you will have trouble. But take heart! I have overcome the world."

Isaiah 58.

Unless otherwise indicated, Bible quotations are taken from the Women's Devotional Bible; New International Version. Copyright © 1990, 1994 by Zondervan Publishing House.

www.ingramcontent.com/pod-product-compliance
Lightning Source LLC
Chambersburg PA
44118CB00036B/2131